This journal belongs to

....

You are a beautiful woman of God,
precious to Him in every way. As you seek Him,
you will find His wonderful promises hold true—
they are a firm foundation on which to stand.

Have confidence in the Lord for He is true to His Word;
He is ever and always the same. Let this journal
inspire you to express your thoughts, embrace your dreams,
record your prayers, and listen to what God is saying to you.

Be strong in the Lord, and rest securely on His promises.

He who promised is faithful.

HEBREWS 10:23 NIV

God's
Promises
FOR A
Woman's Heart

A PROMISE JOURNAL

...*inspired by life*

God's Unfailing Promises

Jesus Christ opens wide the doors of the treasure house
of God's promises, and bids us go in and take with boldness
the riches that are ours.

CORRIE TEN BOOM

Not one word of all the good words which
the LORD your God spoke concerning you has failed;
all have been fulfilled for you, not one of them has failed.

JOSHUA 23:14 NASB

The fulfillment of God's promise depends entirely
on trusting God and his way, and then simply embracing him
and what he does. God's promise arrives as pure gift.

ROMANS 4:16 THE MESSAGE

Faith in God is not blind.
It is based on His character and His promises.

God is the God of promise. He keeps His word, even when
that seems impossible; even when the circumstances
seem to point to the opposite.

COLIN URQUHART

We may...depend upon God's promises, for...He will be
as good as His word. He is so kind that He cannot deceive us,
so true that He cannot break His promise.

MATTHEW HENRY

*Y*our promises have been thoroughly tested;
that is why I love them so much.

PSALM 119:140 NLT

Infinite Love

An infinite God can give all of Himself to each of His children.
He does not distribute Himself that each may have a part,
but to each one He gives all of Himself as fully as if
there were no others.... His love has not changed.
It hasn't cooled off, and it needs no increase because
He has already loved us with infinite love and there is
no way that infinitude can be increased....
He is the same yesterday, today, and forever!

A. W. Tozer

Infinite and yet personal, personal and yet infinite,
God may be trusted because He is the True One.
He is true, He acts truly, and He speaks truly....
God's truthfulness is therefore foundational
for His trustworthiness.

Os Guinness

At the very heart and foundation of all God's dealings with us,
however dark and mysterious they may be, we must dare
to believe in and assert the infinite, unmerited,
and unchanging love of God.

L. B. Cowman

Take a long, hard look. See how great he is—infinite,
greater than anything you could ever imagine or figure out!

JOB 36:26 THE MESSAGE

Overflowing Praise

For great is the LORD, and greatly to be praised,
and he is to be held in awe above all gods.

1 CHRONICLES 16:25 ESV

All enjoyment spontaneously overflows into praise....
The world rings with praise-lovers praising their beloved,
readers their favorite poet, walkers praising the countryside,
players praising their favorite games....

Just as people spontaneously praise what they value,
so they spontaneously urge us to join them in praising it:
"Isn't she lovely? Wasn't it glorious?
Don't you think that was magnificent?..."

I think we delight to praise what we enjoy because
the praise not merely expresses but completes the enjoyment;
it is its appointed consummation.

C. S. LEWIS

God's pursuit of praise from us and our pursuit
of pleasure in Him are one and the same pursuit.
God's quest to be glorified and our quest to be satisfied
reach their goal in this one experience:
our delight in God which overflows in praise.

JOHN PIPER

Earth, with her thousand voices, praises God.

SAMUEL TAYLOR COLERIDGE

Oh, sing to the Lord a new song!
Sing to the Lord, all the earth.

Psalm 96:1 NKJV

A Promise of New Life

For God is, indeed, a wonderful Father who longs
to pour out His mercy upon us, and whose majesty is so great
that He can transform us from deep within.

TERESA OF AVILA

To pray is to change. This is a great grace. How good of God
to provide a path whereby our lives can be taken over by love
and joy and peace and patience and kindness and goodness
and faithfulness and gentleness and self-control.

RICHARD J. FOSTER

Every day we live is a priceless gift of God,
loaded with possibilities to learn something new,
to gain fresh insights.

DALE EVANS ROGERS

You have chosen to bless my family.... LORD,
you have blessed my family, so it will always be blessed.

1 CHRONICLES 17:27 NCV

A life transformed by the power of God is always
a marvel and a miracle.

GERALDINE NICHOLAS

*Create in me a clean heart, O God;
and renew a steadfast spirit within me.*

PSALM 51:10 NKJV

God Is for You

So, what do you think? With God on our side like this,
how can we lose? If God didn't hesitate to put everything
on the line for us, embracing our condition
and exposing himself to the worst by sending his own Son,
is there anything else he wouldn't gladly and freely do for us?
And who would dare tangle with God by messing
with one of God's chosen? Who would dare even
to point a finger? The One who died for us—
who was raised to life for us!—is in the presence
of God at this very moment sticking up for us.

ROMANS 8:31–34 THE MESSAGE

God never abandons anyone on whom
He has set His love; nor does Christ, the good Shepherd,
ever lose track of His sheep.

J. I. PACKER

God...will take care of you day and night forever.

NORMAN VINCENT PEALE

*God's forgiveness and love exist for you as if
you were the only person on earth.*

CECIL OSBORNE

A Heart Full of Gratitude

Gratitude unlocks the fullness of life. It turns what
we have into enough, and more.... It can turn a meal
into a feast, a house into a home, a stranger into a friend.
Gratitude makes sense of our past, brings peace for today,
and creates a vision for tomorrow.

MELODY BEATTIE

Thank the Lord because he is good.
His love continues forever.

1 CHRONICLES 16:34 NCV

Being grateful for what we have today doesn't mean
we have to have that forever. It means we acknowledge that
what we have today is what we're supposed to have today.
There is enough.... And all we need will come to us.

Enter His gates with thanksgiving
And His courts with praise.
Give thanks to Him, bless His name.

PSALM 100:4 NASB

True gratitude, like true love,
must find expression in acts, not words.

R. MILDRED BARKER

*P*raise the Lord and worship him.
Tell everyone what he has done and how great he is.

ISAIAH 12:4 NCV

God's Guidance

To You, O LORD, I lift up my soul.
O my God, in You I trust....
Make me know Your ways, O LORD;
Teach me Your paths.
Lead me in Your truth and teach me,
for You are the God of my salvation;
for You I wait all the day.
Remember, O LORD, Your compassion and
Your lovingkindnesses,
For they have been from of old.

PSALM 25:1–2, 4–6 NASB

Incredible as it may seem, God wants our companionship.
He wants to have us close to Him. He wants to be
a father to us, to shield us, to protect us, to counsel us,
and to guide us in our way through life.

BILLY GRAHAM

The LORD will guide you always;
he will satisfy your needs in a sun-scorched land....
You will be like a well-watered garden,
like a spring whose waters never fail.

ISAIAH 58:11 NIV

*Abandon yourself to His care and guidance, as a sheep
in the care of a shepherd, and trust Him utterly.*

HANNAH WHITALL SMITH

Love One Another

You who have received so much love share it with others.
Love others the way that God has loved you, with tenderness.

MOTHER TERESA

Let Jesus be in your heart,
Eternity in your spirit,
The world under your feet,
The will of God in your actions.
And let the love of God shine forth from you.

CATHERINE OF GENOA

Every single act of love bears the imprint of God.

Love the LORD your God...do what he wants you to do,
and...keep his commands, his rules, and his laws.
Then you will live...and the LORD your God will bless you.

DEUTERONOMY 30:16 NCV

Around me when I look
His handiwork I see;
This world is like a picture book
To teach His love to me.

JANE E. LEESON

*B*eloved, if God so loved us, we also ought to
love one another.... If we love one another,
God abides in us and his love is perfected in us.

1 JOHN 4:11–12 ESV

God's Nearness

Whom have I in heaven but You?
And besides You, I desire nothing on earth.
My flesh and my heart may fail,
But God is the strength of my heart and my portion forever....
As for me, the nearness of God is my good;
I have made the Lord GOD my refuge.

PSALM 73:25–26, 28 NASB

I have sought Thy nearness;
With all my heart have I called Thee,
And going out to meet Thee
I found Thee coming toward me.

YEHUDA HALEVI

Draw near to God and He will draw near to you.

JAMES 4:8 NASB

I want them to be strengthened and joined together
with love so that they may be rich in their understanding.
This leads to their knowing fully God's secret, that is,
Christ himself. In him all the treasures of
wisdom and knowledge are safely kept.

COLOSSIANS 2:2–3 NCV

It is God to whom and with whom we travel, and while He is
the End of our journey, He is also at every stopping place.

ELISABETH ELLIOT

Countless Beauties

From the world we see, hear, and touch,
we behold inspired visions that reveal God's glory.
In the sun's light, we catch warm rays of grace and glimpse
His eternal design. In the birds' song, we hear His voice
and it reawakens our desire for Him. At the wind's touch,
we feel His Spirit and sense our eternal existence.

WENDY MOORE

One thing I have asked from the LORD, that I shall seek:
That I may dwell in the house of the LORD
all the days of my life,
To behold the beauty of the LORD
and to meditate in His temple.

PSALM 27:4 NASB

Something deep in all of us yearns for God's beauty,
and we can find it no matter where we are.

SUE MONK KIDD

May God give you eyes to see beauty
only the heart can understand.

Worship the LORD in the beauty of holiness!

PSALM 96:9 NKJV

All the world is an utterance of the Almighty. Its countless beauties, its exquisite adaptations, all speak to you of Him.

PHILLIPS BROOKS

A Work of Art

Each one of us is God's special work of art. Through us,
He teaches and inspires, delights and encourages,
informs and uplifts all those who view our lives.
God, the master artist, is most concerned about expressing
Himself—His thoughts and His intentions—through what He
paints in our character.... [He] wants to paint
a beautiful portrait of His Son in and through your life.
A painting like no other in all of time.

JONI EARECKSON TADA

He who began a good work in you will carry it
on to completion until the day of Christ Jesus.

PHILIPPIANS 1:6 NIV

Whether we are poets or parents or teachers
or artists or gardeners, we must start where we are
and use what we have. In the process of creation
and relationship, what seems mundane and trivial
may show itself to be holy, precious, part of a pattern.

LUCI SHAW

I will give thanks to You, for I am fearfully
and wonderfully made; wonderful are Your works.

PSALM 139:14 NASB

Satisfaction Guaranteed

God is not only the answer to a thousand needs,
He is the answer to a thousand wants. He is the fulfillment
of our chief desire in all of life. For whether or not
we've ever recognized it, what we desire is unfailing love.
Oh, God, awake our souls to see—You are what we want,
not just what we need. Yes, our life's protection, but also our
heart's affection. Yes, our soul's salvation, but also our heart's
exhilaration. Unfailing love. A love that will not let me go!

BETH MOORE

Grace to all of you who love our Lord Jesus Christ
with love that never ends.

EPHESIANS 6:24 NCV

The greatest honor we can give God is to live gladly
because of the knowledge of His love.

JULIAN OF NORWICH

$\mathcal{S}$atisfy us in the morning with your unfailing love,
that we may sing for joy and be glad all our days.

PSALM 90:14 NIV

Knowing Him More

With God, life is eternal—both in quality and length.
There is no joy comparable to the joy of discovering
something new from God, about God. If the continuing life
is a life of joy, we will go on discovering, learning.

EUGENIA PRICE

This life is not all. It is an "unfinished symphony"…
with those who know that they are related to God
and have felt the power of an endless life.

HENRY WARD BEECHER

I am always with you;
you hold me by my right hand.
You guide me with your counsel,
and afterward you will take me into glory.

PSALM 73:23–24 NIV

Let's praise His name! He is holy, He is almighty.
He is love. He brings hope, forgiveness,
heart cleansing, peace and power. He is our deliverer
and coming King. Praise His wonderful name!

LUCILLE M. LAW

So let us know, let us press on to know the LORD.... He will come to us like the rain, like the spring rain watering the earth.

Joy Is...

Joy is the touch of God's finger. The object of
our longing is not the touch but the Toucher.
This is true of all good things—they are all God's touch.
Whatever we desire, we are really desiring God.

PETER KREEFT

The godly will rejoice in the LORD
and find shelter in him.
And those who do what is right
will praise him.

PSALM 64:10 NLT

Joy is really a road sign pointing us to God.
Once we have found God...we no longer need
to trouble ourselves so much about the quest for joy.

C. S. LEWIS

I will greatly rejoice in the LORD;
my soul shall exult in my God,
for he has clothed me with the garments of salvation;
he has covered me with the robe of righteousness.

ISAIAH 61:10 ESV

Joy is the echo of God's life within us.

May the God of hope fill you with all joy
and peace in believing.

ROMANS 15:13 NKJV

Grace Never Fails

God has not promised skies always blue,
flower-strewn pathways all our lives through;
God has not promised sun without rain,
joy without sorrow, peace without pain.
But God has promised strength for the day,
rest for the labor, light for the way,
grace for the trials, help from above,
unfailing sympathy, undying love.

ANNIE JOHNSON FLINT

For the LORD God is our sun and our shield.
He gives us grace and glory.
The LORD will withhold no good thing
from those who do what is right.

PSALM 84:11 NLT

After winter comes the summer. After night comes the dawn.
And after every storm, there comes clear, open skies.

SAMUEL RUTHERFORD

Those who sow in tears shall reap in joy.

PSALM 126:5 NKJV

Grace...like the Lord, the Giver, never fails from age to age.

JOHN NEWTON

From the fullness of his grace we have all received one blessing after another.

JOHN 1:16 NIV

Shining Promises

Our feelings do not affect God's facts. They may blow up,
like clouds, and cover the eternal things that we do
most truly believe. We may not see the shining
of the promises—but they still shine! [His strength] is not
for one moment less because of our human weakness.

AMY CARMICHAEL

God's ways seem dark, but soon or late,
They touch the shining hills of day.

JOHN GREENLEAF WHITTIER

Tarry at the promise till God meets you there.
He always returns by way of His promises.

L. B. COWMAN

O LORD, God of Israel, there is no God like you in heaven
or on earth—you who keep your covenant of love with your
servants who continue wholeheartedly in your way.

2 CHRONICLES 6:14 NIV

We do not know how this is true—where would faith be
if we did?—but we do know that all things that happen
are full of shining seed. Light is sown for us—not darkness.

*B*ut He knows the way I take; when He has tried me,
I shall come forth as gold.

JOB 23:10 NASB

Go Out in Joy

God infuses...joy from the surprises of life,
which unexpectedly brighten our days,
and fill our eyes with light.

SAMUEL LONGFELLOW

You will go out with joy and be led out in peace.
The mountains and hills will burst into song before you,
and all the trees in the fields will clap their hands.

ISAIAH 55:12 NCV

When we allow God the privilege of shaping our lives,
we discover new depths of purpose and meaning.
What a joyful thought to realize you are
a chosen vessel for God—perfectly suited for His use.

JONI EARECKSON TADA

Love comes while we rest against our Father's chest.
Joy comes when we catch the rhythms of His heart.
Peace comes when we live in harmony with those rhythms.

KEN GIRE

God will yet fill your mouth with laughter
and your lips with shouts of joy.

JOB 8:21 NCV

These things I have spoken to you, that my joy may be in you,
and that your joy may be full.

JOHN 15:11 ESV

Showers of Blessing

Bless the LORD, O my soul;
And all that is within me, bless His holy name!
Bless the LORD, O my soul,
And forget not all His benefits:
Who forgives all your iniquities,
Who heals all your diseases,
Who redeems your life from destruction,
Who crowns you with lovingkindness and tender mercies,
Who satisfies your mouth with good things,
So that your youth is renewed like the eagle's.

PSALM 103:1–5 NKJV

Give thanks for unknown blessings already on their way.

NATIVE AMERICAN PROVERB

I will send down showers in season;
there will be showers of blessing.

EZEKIEL 34:26 NIV

All perfect gifts are from above
and all our blessings show
The amplitude of God's dear love
which any heart may know.

LAURA LEE RANDALL

God, who is love—who is, if I may say it this way, made out of love—simply cannot help but shed blessing on blessing upon us.

HANNAH WHITALL SMITH

The Glow of Love

God is the sunshine that warms us, the rain that melts
the frost and waters the young plants. The presence of God
is a climate of strong and bracing love, always there.

JOAN ARNOLD

May God send His love like sunshine
in His warm and gentle way,
To fill each corner of your heart
each moment of today.

Keep yourselves in the love of God, waiting for the mercy
of our Lord Jesus Christ that leads to eternal life.

JUDE 1:21 ESV

Lord, let the glow of Your love
Through my whole being shine,
Fill me with gladness from above
and hold me by strength Divine;
Lord, make Your Light in my Heart
Glow radiant and clear, never to part.

MARGARET FISHBACK POWERS

No sun, no crown of gold is more radiant than God's love.

CHRISTOPHER DE VINCK

For God is sheer beauty, all-generous in love,
loyal always and ever.

PSALM 100:5 THE MESSAGE

A Present Help

God is our refuge and strength,
an ever-present help in trouble.
Therefore we will not fear, though the earth give way
and the mountains fall into the heart of the sea....
The LORD Almighty is with us;
The God of Jacob is our fortress.

PSALM 46:1–2, 7 NIV

God wants nothing from us except our needs,
and these furnish Him with room to display His bounty
when He supplies them freely.... Not what I have,
but what I do not have, is the first point of contact
between my soul and God.

CHARLES H. SPURGEON

Trust the Lord; he is your helper and your protection.

PSALM 115:9 NCV

Be assured, if you walk with Him and look to Him
and expect help from Him, He will never fail you.

GEORGE MÜELLER

Call upon me in the day of trouble;
I will deliver you, and you will honor me.

PSALM 50:15 NIV

esus Christ has brought every need, every joy,
every gratitude, every hope of ours before God.
He accompanies us and brings us into the presence of God.

DIETRICH BONHOEFFER

Held in His Hand

The mystery of life is that the Lord of life cannot be known
except in and through the act of living. Without the concrete
and specific involvements of daily life we cannot come
to know the loving presence of Him who holds us
in the palm of His hand.... Therefore, we are called
each day to present to our Lord the whole of our lives.

HENRI J. M. NOUWEN

God promises to keep us in the palm of His hand, with or
without our awareness. God has already made a space for us,
even if we have not made a space for God.

DAVID AND BARBARA SORENSEN

He will feed his flock like a shepherd.
He will carry the lambs in his arms,
holding them close to his heart.
He will gently lead the mother sheep with their young.

ISAIAH 40:11 NLT

That Hand which bears all nature up
Shall guard His children well.

WILLIAM COWPER

*B*ehold, I have inscribed you on the palms of My hands.

Surrounded by His Goodness

The light of God surrounds me,
The love of God enfolds me....
The presence of God watches over me,
Wherever I am, God is.

The Lord's goodness surrounds us at every moment.
I walk through it almost with difficulty,
as through thick grass and flowers.

R. W. BARBER

God's love is meteoric,
his loyalty astronomic,
His purpose titanic,
his verdicts oceanic.
Yet in his largeness
nothing gets lost.

PSALM 36:5 THE MESSAGE

He is everything that is good and comfortable for us.
He is our clothing that for love wraps us, clasps us,
and all surrounds us for tender love.

JULIAN OF NORWICH

What can harm us when everything must first touch God
whose presence surrounds us?

We are ever so secure in the everlasting arms.

The LORD is my strength and my shield;
my heart trusted in Him, and I am helped.

PSALM 28:7 NKJV

Mighty to Keep

God is adequate as our keeper.... Your faith will not
fail while God sustains it; you are not strong enough
to fall away while God is resolved to hold you.

J. I. PACKER

Be very careful to observe the commandment and the law
which Moses the servant of the LORD commanded you,
to love the LORD your God and walk in all His ways
and keep His commandments and hold fast to Him
and serve Him with all your heart and with all your soul.

JOSHUA 22:5 NASB

God, who is our dwelling place, is also our fortress.
It can only mean one thing, and that is, that if we will
but live in our dwelling place, we shall be perfectly safe
and secure from every assault.

HANNAH WHITALL SMITH

He who dwells in the shelter of the Most High
will abide in the shadow of the Almighty.

PSALM 91:1–2 NASB

Enfolded in Peace

I will let God's peace infuse every part of today.
As the chaos swirls and life's demands
pull at me on all sides, I will breathe in God's peace
that surpasses all understanding. He has promised that He
would set within me a peace too deeply planted to be affected
by unexpected or exhausting demands.

WENDY MOORE

Calm me, O Lord, as You stilled the storm,
Still me, O Lord, keep me from harm.
Let all the tumult within me cease,
Enfold me, Lord, in Your peace.

CELTIC TRADITIONAL

Don't fret or worry. Instead of worrying, pray.
Let petitions and praises shape your worries into prayers,
letting God know your concerns. Before you know it,
a sense of God's wholeness, everything coming together
for good, will come and settle you down.
It's wonderful what happens when Christ
displaces worry at the center of your life.

PHILIPPIANS 4:6–7 THE MESSAGE

*G*od cannot give us a happiness and peace apart from Himself, because it is not there. There is no such thing.

C. S. LEWIS

Promised Presence

God is with us in the midst of our daily, routine lives.
In the middle of cleaning the house or driving
somewhere in the pickup.... Often it's in the middle
of the most mundane task that He lets us know
He is there with us. We realize, then, that there
can be no "ordinary" moments for people
who live their lives with Jesus.

MICHAEL CARD

God Himself will be with them, and be their God.

REVELATION 21:3 NKJV

Much of what is sacred is hidden in the ordinary,
everyday moments of our lives. To see something
of the sacred in those moments takes slowing down
so we can live our lives more reflectively.

KEN GIRE

We encounter God in the ordinariness of life,
not in the search for spiritual highs and extraordinary,
mystical experiences, but in our simple presence in life.

BRENNAN MANNING

*T*hat's where I'll meet you; that's where I'll speak with you;...
at the place made holy by my Glory.

EXODUS 29:42–43 THE MESSAGE

Finding Joy

Joy is more than my spontaneous expression of laughter,
gaiety, and lightness. It is deeper than an
emotional expression of happiness. Joy is a growing,
evolving manifestation of God in my life as I walk with Him.

BONNIE MONSON

All who seek the LORD will praise him.
Their hearts will rejoice with everlasting joy.

PSALM 22:26 NLT

Happiness is something that comes into our lives
through doors we don't even remember leaving open.

ROSE WILDER LANE

Where does constant joy abound?
In the restless social round,
Entertainment in excess,
Worldly charm or cleverness?
Fleeting are their seeming gains.
Joy is found where Jesus reigns.

HALLIE SMITH BIXBY

Ask and you will receive, so that your joy
will be the fullest possible joy.

JOHN 16:24 NCV

As we grow in our capacities to see and enjoy the joys
that God has placed in our lives, life becomes
a glorious experience of discovering His endless wonders.

God With Us

God gets down on His knees among us; gets on our level
and shares Himself with us. He does not reside afar off
and send diplomatic messages, He kneels among us....
God shares Himself generously and graciously.

EUGENE PETERSON

I love your sanctuary, LORD,
the place where your glorious presence dwells.

PSALM 26:8 NLT

You are in the Beloved...therefore infinitely
dear to the Father, unspeakably precious to Him.
You are never, not for one second, alone.

NORMAN DOWTY

My presence will go with you, and I will give you rest.

EXODUS 33:14 ESV

We are never more fulfilled than when our longing
for God is met by His presence in our lives.

BILLY GRAHAM

God is constantly taking knowledge of me in love,
and watching over me for my good.

J. I. PACKER

You will show me the way of life, granting me the joy of your presence and the pleasures of living with you forever.

PSALM 16:11 NLT

The Goodness of God

All that is good, all that is true, all that is beautiful,
all that is beneficent, be it great or small, be it perfect
or fragmentary, natural as well as supernatural,
moral as well as material, comes from God.

JOHN HENRY NEWMAN

How great is your goodness,
which you have stored up for those who fear you,
which you bestow in the sight of men
on those who take refuge in you.

PSALM 31:19 NIV

We walk without fear, full of hope and courage and strength
to do His will, waiting for the endless good which He is always
giving as fast as He can get us able to take it in.

GEORGE MACDONALD

Open your mouth and taste,
open your eyes and see—
how good GOD is.
Blessed are you who run to him.
Worship GOD if you want the best;
worship opens doors to all his goodness.

PSALM 34:8–9 THE MESSAGE

The goodness of God is infinitely more wonderful
than we will ever be able to comprehend.

The Promise of His Love

A rainbow stretches from one end of the sky to the other.
Each shade of color, each facet of light displays
the radiant spectrum of God's love: a promise that He will
always love each one of us at our worst and at our best.

The King of love my Shepherd is,
Whose goodness faileth never;
I nothing lack if I am His,
And He is mine forever.

SIR HENRY WILLIAMS BAKER

O LORD God of heaven, the great and awesome God
who keeps covenant and steadfast love with those who love
him and keep his commandments, let your ear be attentive
and your eyes open, to hear the prayer of your servant.

NEHEMIAH 1:5 ESV

Faithful, O Lord, Thy mercies are,
A rock that cannot move!
A thousand promises declare
Thy constancy of love.

CHARLES WESLEY

God's love never ceases. Never.... God doesn't love us less
if we fail or more if we succeed. God's love never ceases.

MAX LUCADO

$\mathscr{G}$OD promises to love me all day, sing songs
all through the night! My life is God's prayer.

PSALM 42:8 THE MESSAGE

Special Plans

This is the real gift: you have been given the breath of life,
designed with a unique, one-of-a-kind soul
that exists forever—the way that you choose to live it
doesn't change the fact that you've been given the gift
of being now and forever. Priceless in value,
you are handcrafted by God, who has a personal design
and plan for each of us.

The LORD your God is with you,
he is mighty to save.
He will take great delight in you,
he will quiet you with his love,
he will rejoice over you with singing.

ZEPHANIAH 3:17 NIV

Allow your dreams a place in your prayers and plans.
God-given dreams can help you move
into the future He is preparing for you.

May God's love guide you through
the special plans He has for your life.

The LORD will work out his plans for my life—
for your faithful love, O LORD, endures forever.

PSALM 138:8 NLT

God's Thoughts

Your thoughts—how rare, how beautiful!
God, I'll never comprehend them!
I couldn't even begin to count them—
any more than I could count the sand of the sea.
Oh, let me rise in the morning and live always with you!

PSALM 139:17–18 THE MESSAGE

The counsel of the LORD stands forever,
the plans of his heart to all generations.

PSALM 33:11 ESV

How great are your works, O LORD,
how profound your thoughts!

PSALM 92:5 NIV

"My thoughts are completely different from yours,"
says the LORD. "And my ways are far beyond anything you
could imagine. For just as the heavens are higher
than the earth, so are my ways higher than your ways
and my thoughts higher than your thoughts."

ISAIAH 55:8–9 NLT

Just when we least expect it, He intrudes into our neat
and tidy notions about who He is and how He works.

JONI EARECKSON TADA

Footpath to Peace

To be glad of life, because it gives you the chance to love
and to work and to play and to look up at the stars;
to be satisfied with your possessions, but not contented
with yourself until you have made the best of them...
to think seldom of your enemies, often of your friends,
and every day of Christ; and to spend as much time
as you can, with body and with spirit in God's out-of-doors—
these are little guideposts on the footpath to peace.

HENRY VAN DYKE

But now the LORD my God has given me peace on every side...
and all is well.

1 KINGS 5:4 NLT

Only God gives true peace—a quiet gift He sets within us
just when we think we've exhausted our search for it.

Give me the peace that comes from knowing that where I am,
You are, and together we can handle whatever comes.

PAM KIDD

The LORD will give strength to His people;
The LORD will bless His people with peace.

PSALM 29:11 NKJV

A Promise of Comfort

Blessed be the God and Father of our Lord Jesus Christ,
the Father of mercies and God of all comfort,
who comforts us in all our tribulation, that we may
be able to comfort those who are in any trouble,
with the comfort with which we ourselves
are comforted by God.

2 Corinthians 1:3–4 nkjv

May our Lord Jesus Christ himself and God our Father
encourage you and strengthen you in every good thing you
do and say. God loved us, and through his grace he gave us a
good hope and encouragement that continues forever.

2 Thessalonians 2:16–17 ncv

Blessed is the person who is too busy to worry
in the daytime and too sleepy to worry at night.

Caroline Schroeder

I, even I, am he who comforts you.

Isaiah 51:12 niv

Only God can truly comfort; He comes alongside us
and shows us how deeply and tenderly He feels for us.

The Grace of God

But God, being rich in mercy, because of His
great love with which He loved us, even when we
were dead in our transgressions, made us alive together
with Christ (by grace you have been saved),
and raised us up with Him, and seated us with Him
in the heavenly places in Christ Jesus, so that
in the ages to come He might show the surpassing riches
of His grace in kindness toward us in Christ Jesus.
For by grace you have been saved through faith;
and that not of yourselves, it is the gift of God;
not as a result of works, so that no one may boast.
For we are His workmanship,
created in Christ Jesus for good works,
which God prepared beforehand
so that we would walk in them.

EPHESIANS 2:4–10 NASB

Strength, rest, guidance, grace, help, sympathy, love—
all from God to us! What a list of blessings!

EVELYN STENBOCK

Grace means that God already loves us as much as an infinite God can possibly love.

PHILIP YANCEY

The Blessing of the Lord

The LORD bless you and keep you;
The LORD make His face shine upon you,
And be gracious to you;
The LORD lift up His countenance upon you,
And give you peace.

NUMBERS 6:24–26 NKJV

Drink freely of God's power and experience
His touch of refreshment and blessing.

ANABEL GILLHAM

May the favor of the Lord our God rest upon us;
establish the work of our hands for us—
yes, establish the work of our hands.

PSALM 90:17 NIV

Thank God that even when
we are not worthy of His blessings, He still loves us
and bestows peace, joy, and happiness.

GARY SMALLEY AND JOHN TRENT

Have you ever thought that in every action of grace
in your heart you have the whole omnipotence of God
engaged to bless you?

ANDREW MURRAY

God bless you and utterly satisfy your heart...with Himself.

AMY CARMICHAEL

The Most Beautiful Things

The beauty of the earth, the beauty of the sky,
the order of the stars, the sun, the moon...their very loveliness
is their confession of God, for who made these lovely
mutable things, but He who is Himself unchangeable beauty?

AUGUSTINE

As God's workmanship, we deserve to be treated,
and to treat ourselves, with affection and affirmation,
regardless of our appearance or performance.

MARY ANN MAYO

Your beauty should come from within you—
the beauty of a gentle and quiet spirit that will
never be destroyed and is very precious to God.

1 PETER 3:4 NCV

You are God's created beauty
and the focus of His affection and delight.

JANET WEAVER SMITH

In all ranks of life the human heart yearns
for the beautiful, and the beautiful things that
God makes are His gift to all alike.

HARRIET BEECHER STOWE

The best and most beautiful things in the world cannot be seen or even touched. They must be felt with the heart.

HELEN KELLER

A River of Delights

Your love, O Lord, reaches to the heavens,
your faithfulness to the skies.
Your righteousness is like the mighty mountains,
your justice like the great deep....
How priceless is your unfailing love!
Both high and low among men
find refuge in the shadow of your wings.
They feast on the abundance of your house;
you give them drink from your river of delights.
For with you is the fountain of life;
in your light we see light.

PSALM 36:5–9 NIV

Loving Creator, help me reawaken my childlike
sense of wonder at the delights of Your world!

MARILYN MORGAN HELLEBERG

Joy is perfect acquiesce in God's will because
the soul delights itself in God Himself.

W. WEBB-PEPLOE

Wait and watch for God—
with God's arrival comes love,
with God's arrival comes generous redemption.

PSALM 130:7 THE MESSAGE

God's love is like a river springing up in the Divine Substance and flowing endlessly through His creation, filling all things with life and goodness and strength.

THOMAS MERTON

Always There

We do not need to search for heaven, over here or over there,
in order to find our eternal Father. In fact, we do not
even need to speak out loud, for though we speak
in the smallest whisper or the most fleeting thought,
He is close enough to hear us.

TERESA OF AVILA

How lovely are Your dwelling places, O LORD of hosts!
My soul longed and even yearned for the courts of the LORD;
my heart and my flesh sing for joy to the living God....
For a day in Your courts is better than a thousand outside.

PSALM 84:1–2, 10 NASB

Always be in a state of expectancy, and see that you leave
room for God to come in as He likes.

OSWALD CHAMBERS

God is always present in the temple of your heart...His home. And when you come in to meet Him there, you find that it is the one place of deep satisfaction where every longing is met.

The Promise of His Power

I pray that out of his glorious riches
he may strengthen you with power
through his Spirit in your inner being,
so that Christ may dwell in your hearts through faith.
And I pray that you, being rooted and established in love,
may have power, together with all the saints,
to grasp how wide and long and high and deep is the love of
Christ, and to know this love that surpasses knowledge—
that you may be filled to the measure
of all the fullness of God.

Now to him who is able to do immeasurably more
than all we ask or imagine, according to his power that is
at work within us, to him be glory in the church and
in Christ Jesus throughout all generations,
for ever and ever!
Amen.

EPHESIANS 3:16–21 NIV

When God's power touches a mere human being, something happens! Creation all over again! The life-changing touch of love!

GLORIA GAITHER

Perfect Peace

Let the light of your face shine upon us, O Lord.
You have filled my heart with greater joy
than when their grain and new wine abound.
I will lie down and sleep in peace,
for you alone, O Lord,
make me dwell in safety.

PSALM 4:6–8 NIV

God's peace is joy resting. His joy is peace dancing.

F. F. BRUCE

You keep him in perfect peace whose mind is stayed on you,
because he trusts in you. Trust in the Lord forever,
for the Lord God is an everlasting rock.

ISAIAH 26:3–4 ESV

Joy is not happiness so much as gladness;
it is the ecstasy of eternity in a soul that has made
peace with God and is ready to do His will.

Therefore, having been justified by faith,
we have peace with God through our Lord Jesus Christ.

ROMANS 5:1 NKJV

The God of peace gives perfect peace to those
whose hearts are stayed upon Him.

CHARLES H. SPURGEON

A Purposeful Life

I believe that nothing that happens to me is meaningless,
and that it is good for us all that it should be so,
even if it runs counter to our own wishes. As I see it,
I'm here for some purpose, and I only hope I may fulfill it.

DIETRICH BONHOEFFER

Call to Me, and I will answer you, and show you
great and mighty things, which you do not know.

JEREMIAH 33:3 NKJV

God has a purpose for your life
and no one else can take your place.

Whether you turn to the right or to the left, your ears will
hear a voice behind you, saying, "This is the way; walk in it."

ISAIAH 30:21 NIV

The meaning of earthly existence lies,
not as we have grown used to thinking, in prospering,
but in the development of the soul.

ALEKSANDR SOLZHENITSYN

And we know that all things work together
for good to those who love God, to those who
are the called according to His purpose.

ROMANS 8:28 NKJV

A Splendid Gift

This bright, new day, complete with twenty-four hours
of opportunities, choices, and attitudes comes with
a perfectly matched set of 1440 minutes. This unique gift,
this one day, cannot be exchanged, replaced or refunded.
Handle with care. Make the most of it.
There is only one to a customer!

You have a unique message to deliver,
a unique song to sing, a unique act of love to bestow.
This message, this song, and this act of love
have been entrusted exclusively to the one and only you.

JOHN POWELL, S.J.

Grant me, O God, the power to see
In every rose, eternity;
In every bud, the coming day;
In every snow, the promised May;
In every storm the legacy
Of rainbows smiling down at me!

VIRGINIA WUERFEL

I came that they may have life and have it abundantly.

JOHN 10:10 ESV

Live your life while you have it. Life is a splendid gift—
there is nothing small about it.

FLORENCE NIGHTINGALE

*Isn't everything you have and everything you are
sheer gifts from God?*

1 CORINTHIANS 4:7 THE MESSAGE

Nothing but Grace

There is nothing but God's grace. We walk upon it;
we breathe it; we live and die by it;
it makes the nails and axles of the universe.

ROBERT LOUIS STEVENSON

Grace is no stationary thing, it is ever becoming.
It is flowing straight out of God's heart. Grace does nothing
but re-form and convey God. Grace makes the soul
conformable to the will of God. God, the ground of the soul,
and grace go together.

MEISTER ECKHART

GOD is sheer mercy and grace; not easily angered,
he's rich in love.... As far as sunrise is from sunset,
he has separated us from our sins.

PSALM 103:8, 12 THE MESSAGE

Grace and gratitude belong together like heaven and earth.
Grace evokes gratitude like the voice an echo.
Gratitude follows grace as thunder follows lightning.

KARL BARTH

All those who live with any degree of serenity
live by some assurance of grace.

REINHOLD NIEBUHR

*G*OD is good to one and all;
everything he does is suffused with grace.

PSALM 145:9 THE MESSAGE

Unconditional Love

God says, "I love you no matter what you do."
His love is unconditional and unending.

We are so preciously loved by God that we cannot
even comprehend it. No created being can ever
know how much and how sweetly and tenderly
God loves them. It is only with the help of His grace
that we are able to persevere in...endless wonder at the high,
surpassing, immeasurable love which our Lord
in His goodness has for us.

JULIAN OF NORWICH

The LORD is like a father to his children,
tender and compassionate to those who fear him.
For he knows how weak we are;
he remembers we are only dust.
Our days on earth are like grass;
like wildflowers, we bloom and die.
The wind blows, and we are gone—
as though we had never been here.
But the love of the LORD remains forever
with those who fear him....
The LORD has made the heavens his throne;
from there he rules over everything.

PSALM 103:13–17, 19 NLT

I have loved you with an everlasting love;
I have drawn you with loving-kindness.

Eternal Hope

I pray that your hearts will be flooded with light
so that you can understand the confident hope
he has given to those he called—his holy people
who are his rich and glorious inheritance.

EPHESIANS 1:18 NLT

Hope floods my heart with delight!
Running on air, mad with life, dizzy, reeling,
Upward I mount—faith is sight, life is feeling....
I am immortal! I know it! I feel it!

MARGARET WITTER FULLER

Be strong and let your heart take courage,
all you who hope in the LORD.

PSALM 31:24 NASB

Life is what we are alive to. It is not length but breadth....
Be alive to...goodness, kindness, purity, love, history, poetry,
music, flowers, stars, God, and eternal hope.

MALTBIE D. BABCOCK

For you, O Lord, are my hope,
my trust, O LORD, from my youth.

PSALM 71:5 ESV

Hope sees the invisible, feels the intangible, and achieves the impossible.

Believe His Promises

Faith means being sure of what we hope for...now.
It means knowing something is real, this moment,
all around you, even when you don't see it. Great faith isn't
the ability to believe long and far into the misty future.
It's simply taking God at His word
and taking the next step.

JONI EARECKSON TADA

Now faith is the substance of things hoped for,
the evidence of things not seen.

HEBREWS 11:1 NKJV

You are a child of your heavenly Father. Confide in Him.
Your faith in His love and power can never be bold enough.

BASILEA SCHLINK

Know that the LORD your God is God, the faithful God.
He will keep his agreement of love for a thousand lifetimes
for people who love him and obey his commands.

DEUTERONOMY 7:9 NCV

Within each of us there is an inner place where the living God Himself longs to dwell, our sacred center of belief.

Comfort Sweet

There is a place of comfort sweet
Near to the heart of God,
A place where we our Savior meet,
Near to the heart of God....
Hold us who wait before Thee
Near to the heart of God.

CLELAND B. MCAFEE

Comfort one another, agree with one another, live in peace;
And the God of love and peace shall be with you.

2 CORINTHIANS 13:11 ESV

Not a sigh is breathed, not a pain felt, not a grief
pierces the soul, but the throb vibrates to the Father's heart.

ELLEN G. WHITE

My God loves me, and he goes in front of me.
He will help me defeat my enemies.

PSALM 59:10 NCV

God comforts. He lays His right hand on the wounded soul...
and He says, as if that one were the only soul
in all the universe: O greatly beloved, fear not:
peace be unto thee.

AMY CARMICHAEL

The LORD is my light and my salvation; whom shall I fear?

The Presence of God

I look behind me and you're there,
then up ahead and you're there, too—
your reassuring presence, coming and going.
This is too much, too wonderful—
I can't take it all in!

PSALM 139:5–6 THE MESSAGE

Few delights can equal the mere presence
of one whom we trust utterly.

GEORGE MACDONALD

Where can I go from your Spirit?
Where can I flee from your presence?
If I go up to the heavens, you are there;
if I make my bed in the depths, you are there.
If I rise on the wings of the dawn,
if I settle on the far side of the sea,
even there your hand will guide me,
your right hand will hold me fast.

PSALM 139:7–10 NIV

I am with you and will keep you wherever you go.

GENESIS 28:15 ESV

The Lord's chief desire is to reveal Himself to you and,
in order for Him to do that, He gives you abundant grace.
The Lord gives you the experience of enjoying His presence.

MADAME JEANNE GUYON

Each one of us is encircled by the presence of Almighty God.

CHARLES STANLEY

God's Protection

I've redeemed you. I've called your name. You're mine.
When you're in over your head, I'll be there with you.
When you're in rough waters, you will not go down.
When you're between a rock and a hard place,
it won't be a dead end—Because I am God,
your personal God, The Holy of Israel, your Savior.
I paid a huge price for you...! *That's* how much
you mean to me! *That's* how much I love you!

ISAIAH 43:1–4 THE MESSAGE

If you believe in God, it is not too difficult
to believe that He is concerned about the universe
and all the events on this earth. But the really staggering
message of the Bible is that this same God
cares deeply about you and your identity
and the events of your life.

BRUCE LARSON

If God is for us, who can be against us?

ROMANS 8:31 ESV

*D*o not be afraid to enter the cloud that is settling down on your life. God is in it. The other side is radiant with His glory.

L. B. Cowman

Love All Around

Each day is a treasure box of gifts from God,
just waiting to be opened. Open your gifts with excitement.
You will find forgiveness attached to ribbons of joy.
You will find love wrapped in sparkling gems.

JOAN CLAYTON

I give thanks to GOD with everything I've got....
God's works are so great, worth
A lifetime of study—endless enjoyment!
Splendor and beauty mark his craft;
His generosity never gives out.
His miracles are his memorial—
This GOD of Grace, this God of Love.

PSALM 111:1–4 THE MESSAGE

God give me hope for each day that springs,
God give me joy in the common things!

THOMAS CURTIS CLARK

I am like an olive tree growing in God's Temple.
I trust God's love forever and ever.

PSALM 52:8 NCV

Our God is so wonderfully good, and lovely, and blessed in
every way that the mere fact of belonging to Him is enough
for an untellable fullness of joy!

HANNAH WHITALL SMITH

*L*ove patiently accepts all things. It always trusts,
always hopes, and always endures. Love never ends.

1 CORINTHIANS 13:7–8 NCV

Delight in the Lord

Delight yourself in the LORD
and he will give you the desires of your heart.
Commit your way to the LORD;
trust in him and he will do this:
He will make your righteousness shine like the dawn,
the justice of your cause like the noonday sun.

PSALM 37:4–6 NIV

As we enter more and more deeply into this experience...
our knowledge of God increases, and with it our peace,
our strength and our joy. God help us, then...
that we all may in truth "know the Lord."

J. I. PACKER

Send forth your light and your truth,
let them guide me;
let them bring me to your holy mountain,
to the place where you dwell.
Then will I go to the altar of God,
to God, my joy and my delight.

PSALM 43:3–4 NIV

Our fulfillment comes in knowing God's glory,
loving Him for it, and delighting in it.

*Faith allows us to continually delight in life
since we have placed our needs in God's hands.*

JANET L. WEAVER SMITH

The Beauty of God's Peace

In comparison with this big world, the human heart
is only a small thing. Though the world is so large,
it is utterly unable to satisfy this tiny heart.
Our ever growing soul and its capacities can be satisfied
only in the infinite God. As water is restless until it reaches
its level, so the soul has no peace until it rests in God.

SADHU SUNDAR SINGH

Peace is a margin of power around our daily need.
Peace is a consciousness of springs
too deep for earthly droughts to dry up.

HARRY EMERSON FOSDICK

Let the peace that Christ gives control your thinking,
because you were all called together in one body
to have peace. Always be thankful.

COLOSSIANS 3:15 NCV

Drop Thy still dews of quietness
till all our strivings cease;
take from our souls the strain and stress,
and let our ordered lives confess
the beauty of Thy peace.

JOHN GREENLEAF WHITTIER

Be still, and know that I am God.

PSALM 46:10 NKJV

All-Sufficient Grace

The LORD longs to be gracious to you;
he rises to show you compassion.
For the LORD is a God of justice.
Blessed are all who wait for him!

ISAIAH 30:18 NIV

God is round about us in Christ on every hand,
with many-sided and all-sufficient grace.
All we need to do is to open our hearts.

OLE HALLESBY

O LORD, be gracious to us; we long for you.
Be our strength every morning,
our salvation in time of distress.

ISAIAH 33:2 NIV

From God, great and small, rich and poor, draw living water
from a living spring, and those who serve Him freely and
gladly will receive grace answering to grace.

THOMAS À KEMPIS

I believe that I shall look upon the goodness of the LORD
in the land of the living!

PSALM 27:13 ESV

*L*ord...give me only Your love and Your grace.
With this I am rich enough, and I have no more to ask.

IGNATIUS OF LOYOLA

Blessings Are Extraordinary Gifts

Some blessings—like rainbows after rain or a friend's
listening ear—are extraordinary gifts waiting
to be discovered in an ordinary day.

All the way my Saviour leads me—
What have I to ask beside?
Can I doubt His tender mercy,
Who through life has been my guide?
Heavenly peace, divinest comfort,
Here by faith in Him to dwell!
For I know, what'er befall me,
Jesus doeth all things well.

FANNY J. CROSBY

I will bless you and make your name great,
so that you will be a blessing.

GENESIS 12:2 ESV

We don't have to be perfect to be a blessing.
We are asked only to be real, trusting in His perfection
to cover our imperfection, knowing that one day
we will finally be all that Christ saved us for
and wants us to be.

GIGI GRAHAM TCHIVIDJIAN

*L*ift up your eyes. Your heavenly Father waits to bless you
in inconceivable ways to make your life
what you never dreamed it could be.

ANNE ORTLUND

Unlimited in Goodness

Before anything else, above all else, beyond everything else,
God loves us. God loves us extravagantly,
ridiculously, without limit or condition.
God is in love with us...God yearns for us.

ROBERTA BONDI

There is no limit to God's love.
It is without measure and its depth cannot be sounded.

MOTHER TERESA

Everything which relates to God is infinite.
We must therefore, while we keep our hearts humble,
keep our aims high. Our highest services are indeed
but finite, imperfect. But as God is unlimited in goodness,
He should have our unlimited love.

HANNAH MORE

Love and truth belong to God's people;
goodness and peace will be theirs.
On earth people will be loyal to God,
and God's goodness will shine down from heaven.
The Lord will give his goodness,
and the land will give its crops.
Goodness will go before God
and prepare the way for him.

PSALM 85:10–13 NCV

I lavish unfailing love for a thousand generations
on those who love me and obey my commands.

EXODUS 20:6 NLT

God-Provision

Walk into the fields and look at the wildflowers.
They don't fuss with their appearance—
but have you ever seen color and design quite like it?
The ten best-dressed men and women in the country
look shabby alongside them. If God gives such attention
to the wildflowers, most of them never even seen,
don't you think he'll attend to you, take pride in you,
do his best for you?

What I'm trying to do here is get you to relax,
not be so preoccupied with getting so you can respond
to God's giving. People who don't know God
and the way he works fuss over these things,
but you know both God and how he works.
Steep yourself in God-reality,
God-initiative, God-provisions.
You'll find all your everyday human concerns
will be met. Don't be afraid of missing out.
You're my dearest friends!
The Father wants to give you the very kingdom itself.

LUKE 12:26–32 THE MESSAGE

At the very heart of the universe
is God's desire to give and to forgive.

Our Faithful Father

You, O God, are both tender and kind,
not easily angered, immense in love,
and you never, never quit.

PSALM 86:15 THE MESSAGE

It is good to give thanks to the LORD
and to sing praises to Your name, O Most High;
to declare Your lovingkindness in the morning
and Your faithfulness by night.

PSALM 92:1–2 NASB

For the LORD God is a sun and shield;
The LORD gives grace and glory;
No good thing does He withhold
from those who walk uprightly.

PSALM 84:11 NASB

The LORD is righteous...He will do no injustice. Every morning
He brings His justice to light; He does not fail.

ZEPHANIAH 3:5 NASB

How blessed is the one whom You choose and bring near to You
To dwell in Your courts
We will be satisfied with the goodness of Your house,
Your holy temple.

PSALM 65:4 NASB

God takes care of His own.... At just the right moment
He steps in and proves Himself as our faithful heavenly Father.

CHARLES R. SWINDOLL

Encouragement for Your Heart

The Scriptures give us hope and encouragement as we wait
patiently for God's promises to be fulfilled.

ROMANS 15:4 NLT

When you come looking for me, you'll find me.
Yes, when you get serious about finding me
and want it more than anything else, I'll make sure
you won't be disappointed.... I'll turn things around for you....
Bring you home.... You can count on it.

JEREMIAH 29:13–14 THE MESSAGE

We are of such value to God that He came to live among us...
and to guide us home.

CATHERINE OF SIENNA

When we take time to notice the simple things in life, we
never lack for encouragement. We discover we are surrounded
by a limitless hope that's just wearing everyday clothes.

WENDY MOORE

I will go before you and make the rough places smooth.

ISAIAH 45:2 NASB

O LORD, you are my God; I will exalt you;
I will praise your name, for you have done wonderful things,
plans formed of old, faithful and sure.

ISAIAH 25:1 ESV

Made for Joy

Our hearts were made for joy. Our hearts were made
to enjoy the One who created them. Too deeply planted
to be much affected by the ups and downs of life,
this joy is a knowing and a being known by our Creator.
He sets our hearts alight with radiant joy.

If one is joyful, it means that one is faithfully living
for God, and that nothing else counts; and if one
gives joy to others one is doing God's work.
With joy without and joy within, all is well.

JANET ERSKINE STUART

The joy of the LORD is your strength.

NEHEMIAH 8:10 NKJV

Live for today but hold your hands open to tomorrow.
Anticipate the future and its changes with joy.
There is a seed of God's love in every event,
every circumstance, every unpleasant situation
in which you may find yourself.

BARBARA JOHNSON

But joyful are those who have the God of Israel as their helper,
whose hope is in the LORD their God.

PSALM 146:5 NLT

In God's Thoughts

O LORD, our Lord,
how majestic is your name in all the earth!
You have set your glory
above the heavens....
When I consider your heavens,
the work of your fingers,
the moon and the stars,
which you have set in place,
what is man that you are mindful of him,
the son of man that you care for him?
You made him a little lower than the heavenly beings
and crowned him with glory and honor....
O LORD, our Lord,
how majestic is your name in all the earth!

PSALM 8:1, 3–5, 9 NIV

All God's glory and beauty come from within,
and there He delights to dwell. His visits there are frequent,
His conversation sweet, His comforts refreshing,
His peace passing all understanding.

THOMAS À KEMPIS

We have been in God's thought from all eternity,
and in His creative love, His attention never leaves us.

MICHAEL QUOIST

*Savor little glimpses of God's goodness and His majesty,
thankful for the gift of them.*

All Is Well

A living, loving God can and does make His presence felt,
can and does speak to us in the silence of our hearts,
can and does warm and caress us till we no longer doubt
that He is near, that He is here.

BRENNAN MANNING

If God is present at every point in space, if we cannot go
where He is not, cannot even conceive of a place where
He is not, why then has not that Presence become
the one unanswerably celebrated fact of the world?...
People do not know if God is here. What a difference
it would make if they knew.

A. W. TOZER

We are always in the presence of God.... There is never
a nonsacred moment! His presence never diminishes.
Our awareness of His presence may falter, but the reality
of His presence never changes.

MAX LUCADO

I love the LORD because he hears my voice
and my prayer for mercy.
Because he bends down to listen,
I will pray as long as I have breath!

PSALM 116:1–2 NLT

*B*efore me, even as behind,
God is, and all is well.

JOHN GREENLEAF WHITTIER

God Our Father

Tuck this thought into your heart today. Treasure it.
Your Father God cares about your
daily everythings that concern you.

KAY ARTHUR

God is every moment totally aware of each one of us.
Totally aware in intense concentration and love....
No one passes through any area of life, happy or tragic,
without the attention of God.

EUGENIA PRICE

As a rose fills a room with its fragrance,
so will God's love fill our lives.

MARGARET BROWNLEY

God, you are our Father. We're the clay and you're our potter:
All of us are what you made us.

ISAIAH 64:8 THE MESSAGE

God is a rich and bountiful Father, and He does not forget
His children, nor withhold from them anything which it would
be to their advantage to receive.

J. K. MACLEAN

May God our Father and the Lord Jesus Christ
give you grace and peace.

Faithfulness Extended

Remember your promise to me,
it is my only hope.
Your promise revives me;
it comforts me in all my troubles....
I meditate on your age-old regulations;
O Lord, they comfort me....

Your eternal word, O Lord,
stands firm in heaven.
Your faithfulness extends to every generation,
as enduring as the earth you created.
Your regulations remain true to this day.

PSALM 119:49–50, 52, 89–91 NLT

Let love and faithfulness never leave you;
bind them around your neck,
write them on the tablet of your heart.

PROVERBS 3:3 NIV

I know that God is faithful. I know that He answers prayers,
many times in ways I may not understand.

SHEILA WALSH

*S*wim through your troubles. Run to the promises,
they are our Lord's branches hanging over the water
so that His children may take a grip of them.

SAMUEL RUTHERFORD

Fresh Hope

God...rekindles burned-out lives with fresh hope,
restoring dignity and respect to their lives—
a place in the sun! For the very structures of earth are GOD's;
he has laid out his operations on a firm foundation.

1 SAMUEL 2:7–8 THE MESSAGE

Hope is some extraordinary spiritual grace that God gives us
to control our fears, not to oust them.

VINCENT MCNABB

I will praise you forever for what you have done;
in your name I will hope, for your name is good.
I will praise you in the presence of your saints.

PSALM 52:9 NIV

The hope we have in Christ is an absolute certainty.
We can be sure that the place Christ is preparing for us
will be ready when we arrive, because with Him nothing is
left to chance. Everything He promised He will deliver.

BILLY GRAHAM

Though seen through many a tear,
Let not my star of hope grow dim or disappear.

BENJAMIN SCHMOLCK

Known By Him

The simple fact of being...in the presence of the Lord
and of showing Him all that I think, feel, sense,
and experience, without trying to hide anything,
must please Him. Somehow, somewhere, I know that
He loves me, even though I do not feel that love
as I can feel a human embrace, even though I do not hear
a voice as I hear human words of consolation....
God is greater than my senses, greater than my thoughts,
greater than my heart. I do believe that He touches me
in places that are unknown even to myself.

HENRI J. M. NOUWEN

Pour out your heart to God your Father.
He understands you better than you do.

It is in silence that God is known,
and through mysteries that He declares Himself.

ROBERT H. BENSON

If anyone loves God, this one is known by Him.

1 CORINTHIANS 8:3 NKJV

God's Peace

Let not your heart be troubled; you believe in God,
believe also in Me. In My Father's house are many mansions;
if it were not so, I would have told you. I go to prepare
a place for you. And if I go and prepare a place for you,
I will come again and receive you to Myself; that where I am,
there you may be also....

I will not leave you...; I will come to you.... Peace I leave
with you, My peace I give to you; not as the world gives
do I give to you. Let not your heart be troubled,
neither let it be afraid.

JOHN 14:1–3, 18, 27 NKJV

Stand outside this evening. Look at the stars. Know that
you are special and loved by the One who created them.

God will never let you be shaken or moved
from your place near His heart.

JONI EARECKSON TADA

May the God of love and peace set your heart at rest
and speed you on your journey.

RAYMOND OF PENYAFORT

Divine Romance

God's holy beauty comes near you, like a spiritual scent,
and it stirs your drowsing soul.... He creates in you
the desire to find Him and run after Him—to follow wherever
He leads you, and to press peacefully against His heart
wherever He is. If you are seeking after God, you may be sure
of this: God is seeking you much more. He is the Lover,
and you are His beloved. He has promised Himself to you.

JOHN OF THE CROSS

To fall in love with God is the greatest of all romances—
to seek Him the greatest of all adventures, to find Him the
greatest human achievement.

AUGUSTINE

God's eye is on those who respect him,
the ones who are looking for his love.
He's ready to come to their rescue in bad times;
in lean times he keeps body and soul together.

PSALM 33:18 THE MESSAGE

In the morning let our hearts gaze upon God's love...and in
the beauty of that vision, let us go forth to meet the day.

ROY LESSIN

*N*othing in all creation will ever be able
to separate us from the love of God.

ROMANS 8:39 NLT

Rest in Him

My soul finds rest in God alone;
my salvation comes from him.
He alone is my rock and my salvation;
he is my fortress, I will never be shaken....
My salvation and my honor depend on God;
he is my mighty rock, my refuge.
Trust in him at all times, O people;
pour out your hearts to him,
for God is our refuge....
One thing God has spoken,
two things have I heard:
that you, O God, are strong,
and that you, O Lord, are loving.

PSALM 62:1–2, 7–8, 11–12 NIV

Joy comes from knowing God loves me
and knows who I am and where I'm going...
that my future is secure as I rest in Him.

JAMES DOBSON

Rest in the Lord, and wait patiently for him.

PSALM 37:7 NASB

When God finds a soul that rests in Him and is not easily
moved...to this same soul He gives the joy of His presence.

CATHERINE OF GENOA

Uniquely Loved

Show the wonder of your great love....
Keep me as the apple of your eye;
hide me in the shadow of your wings.

PSALM 17:7–8 NIV

All the things in this world are gifts and signs
of God's love to us. The whole world is a love letter from God.

PETER KREEFT

Give thanks to the LORD, for he is good!
His faithful love endures forever.

PSALM 136:1 NLT

God has a wonderful plan for each person He has chosen.
He knew even before He created this world what beauty
He would bring forth from our lives.

LOUIS B. WYLY

The LORD is gracious and merciful,
slow to anger and abounding in steadfast love....
The LORD is faithful in all his words
and kind in all his works.

PSALM 145:8, 13 ESV

There is the whisper of His love, the joy of His presence, and the shining of His face, for those who love Jesus for Himself alone.

SUSAN B. STRACHAN

A Place of Rest

Knowest thou not that day follows night, that flood
comes after ebb, that spring and summer succeed winter?
Hope thou then! Hope thou ever! God fails thee not.

CHARLES H. SPURGEON

God provides resting places as well as working places.
Rest, then, and be thankful when He brings you,
wearied to a wayside well.

L. B. COWMAN

In those times I can't seem to find God,
I rest in the assurance He knows how to find me.

NEVA COYLE

As for me, I trust in You, O LORD,
I say, "You are my God."
My times are in Your hand.

PSALM 31:14–15 NASB

Wait upon God's strengthening, and say to Him,
"O Lord, You have been our refuge in all generations."
Trust in Him who has placed this burden on you.
What you yourself cannot bear, bear with the help
of God who is all-powerful.

BONIFACE

*L*ord, You have been our dwelling place in all generations....
Even from everlasting to everlasting, You are God.

PSALM 90:1–2 NASB

Good Plans

Remember the things I have done in the past.
For I alone am God!
I am God, and there is none like me.
Only I can tell you the future
before it even happens.
Everything I plan will come to pass.

ISAIAH 46:9–10 NLT

"For I know the plans I have for you," declares the LORD,
"plans to prosper you and not to harm you,
plans to give you hope and a future."

JEREMIAH 29:11 NIV

Even when all we see are the tangled threads
on the backside of life's tapestry, we know that God
is good and is out to do us good always.

RICHARD J. FOSTER

No eye has seen, nor ear heard,
nor the heart of man imagined,
what God has prepared for those who love him.

1 CORINTHIANS 2:9 ESV

*E*very person's life is a fairy tale written by God's fingers.

HANS CHRISTIAN ANDERSEN

Wonderful Joy

Be truly glad! There is wonderful joy ahead....
You love him even though you have never seen him.
Though you do not see him now, you trust him;
and you rejoice with a glorious, inexpressible joy.

1 PETER 1:6, 8–9 NLT

Your deepest joy comes when you have nothing around you
to bring outward pleasure and Jesus becomes your total joy.

A. WETHERELL JOHNSON

The ransomed of the LORD will return. They will enter Zion
with singing; everlasting joy will crown their heads.
Gladness and joy will overtake them,
and sorrow and sighing will flee away.

ISAIAH 35:10 NIV

Herein is joy, amid the ebb and flow of the passing world:
our God remains unmoved, and His throne endures forever.

ROBERT COLEMAN

Rejoice always, pray without ceasing, in everything give
thanks; for this is the will of God in Christ Jesus for you.

1 THESSALONIANS 5:16–18 NKJV

Through all eternity to Thee a joyful song I'll raise;
for oh! eternity's too short to utter all Thy praise.

JOSEPH ADDISON

His Compassions Never Fail

Through the LORD's mercies we are not consumed,
Because His compassions fail not.
They are new every morning;
Great is Your faithfulness.
"The LORD is my portion," says my soul,
"Therefore I hope in Him!"
The LORD is good to those who wait for Him,
To the soul who seeks Him.

LAMENTATIONS 3:22–25, NKJV

Have confidence in God's mercy, for when you think
He is a long way from you, He is often quite near.

THOMAS À KEMPIS

LORD, don't hold back your tender mercies from me.
Let your unfailing love and faithfulness always protect me.

PSALM 40:11 NLT

Whoever walks toward God one step,
God runs toward him two.

JEWISH PROVERB

What counts is whether we have been transformed
into a new creation. May God's peace and mercy be upon all
who live by this principle; they are the new people of God.

GALATIANS 6:15–16 NLT

The loving God we serve has immeasurable compassion
and tenderness toward each of us throughout our lives.

JAMES DOBSON

God's Care

The LORD is my shepherd;
I shall not want.
He makes me to lie down in green pastures;
He leads me beside the still waters.
He restors my soul;
He leads me in the paths of righteousness
For His name's sake.
Yea, though I walk through the valley of the shadow of death,
I will fear no evil; for You are with me;
Your rod and Your staff, they comfort me.
You prepare a table before me in the presence of my enemies;
You anoint my head with oil; my cup runs over.
Surely goodness and mercy shall follow me
All the days of my life:
And I will dwell in the house of the LORD
Forever.

PSALM 23:1–6 NKJV

Leave behind your fear and dwell on the lovingkindness
of God, that you may recover by gazing on Him.

The everlasting God is your place of safety,
and his arms will hold you up forever.

DEUTERONOMY 33:27 NCV

Praise for the Promises

Our thanksgiving today should include those things
which we take for granted, and we should continually
praise our God, who is true to His promise,
who has provided and retained the necessities for our living.

BETTY FUHRMAN

How blessed are the people who know the joyful sound!
O LORD, they walk in the light of Your countenance.
In Your name they rejoice all the day,
And by Your righteousness they are exalted.

PSALM 89:15–16 NASB

May your life become one of glad and unending praise
to the Lord as you journey through this world,
and in the world that is to come!

TERESA OF AVILA

Light shines on the godly,
and joy on those whose hearts are right.
May all who are godly rejoice in the LORD
and praise his holy name!

PSALM 97:11–12 NLT

Our inner happiness depends not on what we
experience but on the degree of our gratitude to God,
whatever the experience.

ALBERT SCHWEITZER

I will bless the LORD at all times:
His praise shall continually be in my mouth.

PSALM 34:1 NKJV

Completely Loved

You are valuable just because you exist. Not because of what
you do or what you have done, but simply because you are.
Just think about the way Jesus honors you...and smile.

MAX LUCADO

We have come to know and to believe the love
that God has for us. God is love, and whoever abides in love
abides in God, and God abides in him.

1 JOHN 4:16 ESV

What good news! God knows me completely and still loves me.

I will rejoice in doing them good, and I will plant them in this
land in faithfulness, with all my heart and all my soul.

JEREMIAH 32:41 ESV

The heart is rich when it is content, and it is always content
when its desires are fixed on God. Nothing can bring greater
happiness than doing God's will for the love of God.

MIGUEL FEBRES CORDERO-MUÑOZ

We love Him, because He first loved us.

1 JOHN 4:19 NKJV

God's Living Word

The word of God is living and active and sharper
than any two-edged sword, and piercing as far
as the division of soul and spirit, of both joints and marrow,
and able to judge the thoughts and intentions of the heart.
And there is no creature hidden from His sight,
but all things are open and laid bare to the eyes
of Him with whom we have to do.

HEBREWS 4:12–13 NASB

With my whole heart have I sought You:
Oh, let me not wander from Your commandments!
Your word I have hidden in my heart,
that I might not sin against You.

PSALM 119:10–11 NKJV

Every part of Scripture is God-breathed and useful
one way or another—showing us truth,
exposing our rebellion, correcting our mistakes,
training us to live God's way. Through the Word we are put
together and shaped up for the tasks God has for us.

2 TIMOTHY 3:16–17 THE MESSAGE

When we give the Word of God space to live in our heart,
the Spirit of God will use it to take root,
penetrating the earthiest recesses of our lives.

KEN GIRE

What Matters

The God who created, names, and numbers the stars
in the heavens also numbers the hairs of my head....
He pays attention to very big things and to very small ones.
What matters to me matters to Him,
and that changes my life.

ELISABETH ELLIOT

What matters supremely is not the fact that I know God,
but the larger fact which underlies it—the fact that
He knows me. I am graven on the palms of His hands.
I am never out of His mind. All my knowledge of Him
depends on His sustained initiative in knowing me. I know
Him because He first knew me, and continues to know me.

J. I. PACKER

One hundred years from today your present income
will be inconsequential. One hundred years from now
it won't matter if you got that big break....
It will greatly matter that you knew God.

DAVID SHIBLEY

I press on so that I may lay hold of that for which
also I was laid hold of by Christ Jesus.

PHILIPPIANS 3:12 NASB

God's Promises for a Woman's Heart

A PROMISE JOURNAL

© 2010 Ellie Claire℠ Gift & Paper Corp.
Minneapolis 55438
www.ellieclaire.com

ISBN 978-1-935416-80-7

Scripture references are from the following sources: The Holy Bible, New International Version® NIV®.
Copyright © 1973, 1978, 1984 by International Bible Society. Used by permission of Zondervan.
The New King James Version (NKJV). Copyright © 1982 by Thomas Nelson, Inc. Used by permission.
The Holy Bible, English Standard Version® (ESV), copyright © 2001 by Crossway Bibles, a publishing
ministry of Good News Publishers. Used by permission. The New American Standard Bible® (NASB),
Copyright © 1960, 1962, 1963, 1968, 1971, 1972, 1973, 1975, 1977, 1995 by The Lockman Foundation.
Used by permission. The Holy Bible, New Living Translation (NLT). Copyright © 1996, 2004.
Used by permission of Tyndale House Publishers, Inc., Wheaton, Illinois. *The Message* © 1993, 1994, 1995,
1996, 2000, 2001, 2002 by Eugene Peterson. Used by permission of NavPress, Colorado Springs, CO.
The New Century Version® (NCV). Copyright © 1987, 1988, 1991 by Thomas Nelson, Inc. Used by permission.
All rights reserved.

Excluding Scripture verses and divine pronouns, in some quotations references to men
and masculine pronouns have been replaced with gender-neutral or feminine references.

Compiled by Jaymie Tomlinson
Cover and interior design by Lisa & Jeff Franke

Printed in China